Tina—

Merry Christmas
2008

Michelle

what a woman needs

Sandy Gingras

**Andrews McMeel
Publishing, LLC**

Kansas City

08 09 10 11 12 TWP 10 9 8 7 6 5 4 3 2

ISBN-13: 978-0-7407-7107-1
ISBN-10: 0-7407-7107-8

Library of Congress Control Number: 2007933997

www.andrewsmcmeel.com

I wrote this book because I needed to. I had a year of stress and change and loss.

As my mother would say, "Welcome to the world; you're not alone..." Still, I found myself feeling overwhelmed and kind of floating—like there was nothing to hold onto anymore. I knew I had to do something. I decided to get back to the basics— not only to simplify my life, but to simplify myself.

I started making a list (which is what I do in times of stress) of what I needed in my life, what I considered the essentials. It struck me, as I was writing, how much I had forgotten about life in the process of living; how much I had forgotten about myself because life got complicated and busy. And how much I had focused my life on what I wanted (or thought I wanted) instead of what I needed.

This is a book of simple things: moments, emotions, gestures (from the silly to the sublime). But that's because I realized (or remembered) that what we really need in life is simple. Most of what we need is within us or right in front of us. Most of it is free. Most of it isn't things at all. And most of it, we already have.

This book reminded me of how full my life really is. It made me feel happy and thankful to write it. I hope it gives you that feeling too...

what a woman needs

to nest

to be seen through

an elastic waistband

garbage day

to be in over her head

to stop and smell the flowers

good lighting

old friends

to learn

to sit down

more
endorphins
please

to launch her dreams

to let go

of the small stuff

hope

a night-light

to loosen up

to feel beautiful

to put her feet up

the idea of a lifeguard

just the facts ma'am

to slow down

a little mystery

a big umbrella

when the sky is falling

her own personal space

an off switch

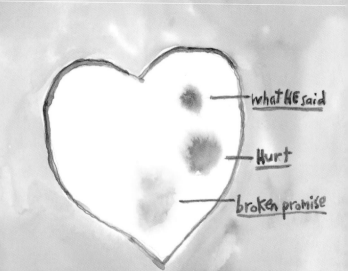

what HE said

Hurt

broken promise

stain remover

to smile more

to bewitch

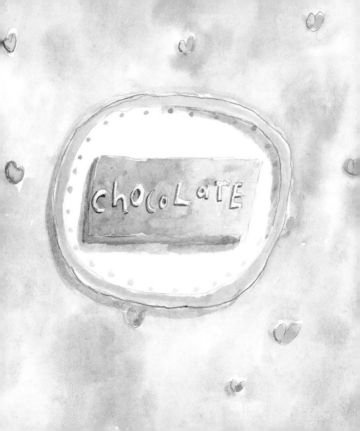

to believe in herself

to wine

to belly laugh

to outgrow her container

to balance

(although the world is uneven)

support

a jump start

a door opening

to hold on

to the simple things

to be understood

to know that when the tide goes out,
it will come back in again

to feed her heart

to be a part of
something bigger

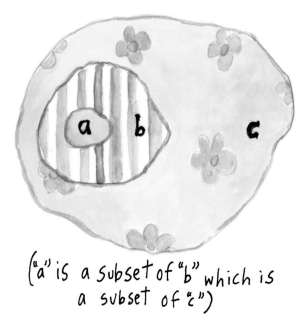

("a" is a subset of "b" which is
a subset of "c")

to come undone

to throw herself in

a wind shift

to escape from

her own head

to weather some storms

to seek answers

to be touched

to be moonstruck

to show her true colors

family

to feel strong

electricity

something to

shoot for

acceptance

to stretch

to melt

You are invited
to...

The Blissful Spa

to escape

words of affection

to be awed

to open up

time to heal

to stand tall

to be asked to dance

to untangle

refreshment

to be swept away

to make friends

with the mood swing

that homey feeling

a little sweetness

to start somewhere